WHERE I COME FROM

Scenes from Abroad
by Mike Williams

Richard Nelson

BROADWAY PLAY PUBLISHING INC
New York
BroadwayPlayPub.com

WHERE I COME FROM
© Copyright 2020 Richard Nelson

First edition: April 2020
I S B N: 978-0-88145-870-1

Book design: Marie Donovan
Page make-up: Adobe InDesign
Typeface: Palatino

WHERE I COME FROM: *Scenes From Abroad By Mike Williams* was commissioned and produced by National Theatre/Shell Connections. It was first presented by The East Norfolk Sixth Form College in the National's Cottesloe Theatre on 10 July 2004.

CHARACTERS

YOUNG MAN, *our narrator, age 16*

DAN, *the teacher's son, 17*
EMILY, *his best friend, 16*
EMMA, *her friend, 17*
RICHARD, *18*
JANE, *his girlfriend, 17*
HENRY, *16*
JAMES, *15*
BILL, *16*
KATHY, *16*
LIBBY, *15*
BECCA, *16*
CAT, *daughter of the owners of the B & B, English, 16*

All the characters, except CAT, *are American*

Prologue

(The sitting room of a Bed & Breakfast, London)

(Chairs, a sofa, end tables, coffee table, lamps, etc. Off to one side is the entryway, and to the other, the stairs to the bedrooms [neither need be seen]. So anyone going from outside to upstairs must snake his way through this room.)

(To one side of the stage—a chair: this is not part of the sitting room.)

(Evening. The lamps are on. Emily sits alone, trying to read, her feet up. She has a box of tissues near her; she is a bit sick and has been sneezing and blowing her nose.)

(A YOUNG MAN *stands and speaks to the audience. He is our narrator and he—like all but one of the characters—is American.)*

YOUNG MAN: *(To us:)* It's January, 1987. And we're but a short walk from the Russell Square Tube stop, on the crescent-shaped street, Cartwright Gardens, home to maybe five or six B & Bs, this being the sitting room of one of them. *(He holds a paperback guidebook [Morton's* Americans In London*].)* There was—and is—much history in these grey streets for Americans. *(Holds up the book and opens it.)* Just around the corner at 5 Woburn Walk, arrived the poet Ezra Pound with the fresh-off-the-boat and very young Robert Frost to a Monday night 'at home' at Mr William Butler Yeats'. It was at this gathering that Mr Frost asked the Irish poet, "Do you really believe in fairies?" *(He turns as page.)* Guildford Street. *(He points it out.)* Where Mark Van

Doren, while living in the 'coldest room in London' got this published in the 'agony' column of *The Times: (Reads:)* "Young American, literary, but interested in everything, desires London friends." *(Turns another page)* Great Russell from where Hemingway wrote his father: "Dear Pappy: I can't think of any more appropriate place to write you from than the reading room of the British Museum with Englishmen as thick as Englishmen and a draft on the back of my neck which I can feel in my balls." *(Turns pages:)* T S Eliot, Ralph Waldo Emerson. Fred Astaire. *(Looks up, then closes the book.)* Unfortunately, none of that has any bearing on our story. Instead, ours is a tale of high school students, from a Philadelphia suburb—you'll meet many of them, the rest are staying at the B & B next door—who are just completing a long hard difficult week—of culture. With the occasional break for shopping to keep their sanity. Tomorrow they go home, so this is their last night. *(He turns to* EMILY.*)* Emily missed the play tonight. She has a cold.

*(*EMILY *sneezes.)*

YOUNG MAN: Her best friend is Dan and he has promised to bring her back a program. Dan's father is Mr Williams, the head teacher for this trip. He and the other two teachers, for reasons unexplained, have rooms at the B & B next door. Here Mr and Mrs Davis, the owners, rule and keep the order. But tonight—

*(*CAT, *16, enters with a cup of hot water and a package of lemonsip for the sick* EMILY.*)*

YOUNG MAN: —they unexpectedly have been called away to the sickbed of Mrs Davis' mother, in Brighton, and so have left their daughter, Caitlin, in charge.

*(*CAT *leaves.)*

YOUNG MAN: Where I Come From. Scenes From Abroad. By—me. Scene One. Home Away From Home.

(The YOUNG MAN *steps aside as we begin to hear voices off—the students returning from the theater.)*

(The YOUNG MAN *will sit in the side chair and watch.)*

Scene One

*(*BECCA, KATHY, *and* LIBBY *enter talking:)*

KATHY: *What* did he say?

LIBBY: Kathy—

KATHY: *(Over this)* What did he say?!

LIBBY: *(To* BECCA*)* I'm sorry I brought it up. I didn't—

KATHY: *(Over the end of this)* Tell me what he said, Libby.

LIBBY: It was nothing. He thought she looked like you.

KATHY: The girl in—

BECCA: In the play.

KATHY: *(Taking out cigarettes)* I don't even like him.

EMILY: *(Over this)* How as the play—?

KATHY: *(Getting her cigarettes)* Which girl in the stupid play? Jesus Christ, the stuck up one?

BECCA: *(Over this to* EMILY*)* How are you feeling?

EMILY: How as the—? *(Sneezes)*

LIBBY: *(To* EMILY*)* Boring. Like very other one. Why would this be any different? Why couldn't I have gotten sick?

KATHY: The girl in the knee-high socks?

LIBBY: I don't know—

KATHY: *(Over this)* I hate those kinds of socks. I'd rather die than—. Who wears—?

BECCA: I don't think he meant—

KATHY: *(A flush of excitement, she now has an excuse to go and confront this boy)* Where is he? Where's Henry? I want to talk to him.

(KATHY Hurries Back Off, BECCA follows.)

LIBBY: *(To EMILY)* Did my mother call?

EMILY: About an hour ago, she said—

LIBBY: I don't care what she said. I know all the shit that she says.

(DAN enters carrying two programs.)

EMILY: Where's my program?!

(DAN holds it up.)

EMILY: How much did it cost?

DAN: A pound fifty.

LIBBY: They really rip you off here.

DAN: They don't rip—

LIBBY: *(To herself)* God I sound like my mother.

(KATHY and BECCA are returning.)

BECCA: He says every cut girl looks like you.

KATHY: When does he—?

EMILY: Where's Henry?

BECCA: The boys are out front being lectured at by Mr Williams.

DAN: I'm a boy and I'm not—

EMILY: What did they do now?

BECCA: I think they tried to sneak away—

KATHY: And Dan's father caught them.

DAN: What my father does has nothing to do with—

BECCA: Who's sensitive??

KATHY: *(To BECCA)* You got a light?

(BECCA *looks through her purse and soon will pull out a lighter.*)

KATHY: What did Henry really say about me?

EMILY: *(To* DAN, *over this, about the program)* I'll pay you back when—. It's nice.

DAN: They are really nice.

EMILY: Where were they sneaking to this time? *(About the smoke)* I have a sore throat. Blow it over there.

KATHY: Some club Henry knows or says he knows about.

DAN: How does Henry know about—?

BECCA: A strip club.

EMILY: Really? Oh that would be right up his—

KATHY: That's what I said. *(She laughs.)*

BECCA: He said he's already been there.

EMILY: When could he have—?

BECCA: He snuck out of the Portrait museum and went.

LIBBY: Maybe what he saw there reminded him of you too, Kathy.

KATHY: *(Smoking)* That—would be okay with me.

(Laughter)

KATHY: Maybe we should go with them. That would freak them out. Where are they, anyway? *(To* BECCA*)* Go look.

(BECCA *goes out.*)

(Short pause)

(KATHY *smokes.*)

EMILY: *(To* KATHY*)* I like that skirt.

LIBBY: It's mine. *(To* KATHY*)* Could I use your lip gloss?

EMILY: I know.

KATHY: I think it should be shorter.

(KATHY *pulls it up a little; throws* LIBBY *her bag so she can find the lip gloss.*)

LIBBY: *(Holding up a little plastic bag)* I got something to—smoke.

KATHY: Where did you—?

LIBBY: *(Over this)* A guy at the tube station, just came up to me. Five pounds.

EMILY: How do you know it's—?

KATHY: Let's try it. Emily?

EMILY: Not tonight. My throat feels—

KATHY: We won't even bother asking Dan. We know what he'd say.

DAN: What would I say?

(Over this, voices off as some of the boys are entering:)

HENRY: Who the fuck does he think he is?

(BILL, HENRY, *and* JAMES *enter, angry.* BECCA *follows.*)

HENRY: *(Turns to* DAN) Your father, Dan, what is wrong with him?

DAN: I don't know. I really don't know.

KATHY: What did he—?

HENRY: He's screaming at us. What were we going to do? He has no idea what we were going to do. We hadn't done anything yet. He's guessing. He's an idiot.

DAN: I know. I know.

JAMES: He threatened to call our parents. *(Sees the plastic bag)* What's that?

LIBBY: *(Hiding it and flirting)* It's not for you. There's not enough. *(To* KATHY*)* We were on our way upstairs, weren't we? Becca?

BECCA: I'm coming.

KATHY: *(To* HENRY*)* I hear you thought someone looked like me?

HENRY: Who told you that? Yeh.

KATHY: One of the actresses. She looked like—?

HENRY: Yeh. *(To the others)* What was that play about anyway? I didn't get it.

KATHY: Why did she look like me?

*(*HENRY *shrugs.)*

KATHY: Because she was ugly like me?

*(*KATHY *smiles, can't resist a tickle and runs off up the stairs.* BECCA *and* LIBBY *hurry after.)*

*(*HENRY *turns to* JAMES *and hits him hard with his fist on the shoulder.* JAMES *hits him back.)*

HENRY: *(To* DAN*)* Your Dad's a moron.

DAN: I know that. I do. He's an incredible moron.

JAMES: You know it's probably birdseed she bought. She thinks it's—. But it's birdseed.

BILL: Or oregano.

*(*JANE *and* RICHARD *enter.)*

BILL: *(To* JAMES*)* Give me one of your cigarettes.

RICHARD: *(Over this)* What's got up Mr Williams' ass?

JANE: He was out there shout at us—

JAMES: *(At the same time)* He was screaming at us.

RICHARD: *(At the same time)* We didn't' do anything. Jane and I took a walk around the square. "Where have you been? What have you been doing?" What has gotten into him?

(They all are headed toward the stairs.)

HENRY: What did *I* do? I watched every goddamn stupid play. I haven't complained much. Lay off me, man!

(They are gone. DAN and EMILY are alone.)

DAN: He gets this way sometimes. My father. What time is it where we come from?

EMILY: It's still the middle of the afternoon.

DAN: So my Mom's not home from work yet. So it couldn't be her. Sometimes when he talks to her…

(EMILY takes a sip of her lemonsip.)

EMILY: This stuff really works. We should take some home.

DAN: Yeh.

EMILY: Want a sip?

(DAN starts to take one, then stops.)

DAN: Aren't you… *(sick)*?

EMILY: Right. That was close.

(Music is turned on upstairs.)

EMILY: They found a station that isn't just talk.

EMILY: *(Fiddling with the program)* So how was this play? *(Reads the title:)* Misalliance.

DAN: It was okay.

EMILY: What does the title…?

DAN: I don't know. A plane flies into this house.

EMILY: They showed that?

DAN: Yeh. It flew into a big picture window.

EMILY: Wow.

DAN: Yeh.

(DAN *looks at the program with* EMILY, *then:*)

DAN: It didn't work tonight. It broke.

EMILY: What do you mean it—?

DAN: It started to fly into the—. But it got stuck on something. Just sort of... They had to stop the show. When they started up again, the actors said some of the lines they'd already said—so they went back a little—it was weird. I don't know why they did that. But you could tell that it would have been neat. The plan.

EMILY: Yeh.

DAN: My father loved it. "The Royal Shakespeare Company". He loves all that stuff.

EMILY: He has to. He's as teacher.

DAN: Right.

(DAN *and* EMILY *look at the program.*)

EMILY: Did you walk there or take the tube.

DAN: We took the tube.

EMILY: I'm sorry I missed that. I love the tube.

DAN: But the theatre's in a real strange place. Really— ugly. You think of England and you think -. But this was—ugly. And confusing. The Barbican. It means something. I don't know what. And I don't care. (*Laughs to himself*) We got lost like three times. Twice getting there. And again coming home. Even my father. And he's been here...

EMILY: Did you walk behind him and make those faces. (*She mimics him making faces.*)

DAN: I don't always do that.

EMILY: *(Over the end of this)* You know that won't make them like you any more.

DAN: That's not why I—

EMILY: And who cares what they think.

DAN: That's not why I do that. And anyway, they like me. It's my Dad they don't like.

EMILY: True.

(CAT enters talking, wiping her hand on her apron. She has been doing the dishes.)

(The lights start to fade.)

CAT: And how is the patient—?

EMILY: It's already working I think, Cat. My throat feels better. *(To DAN)* It has something like aspirin in it too.

CAT: *(To DAN)* It's what I always take.

DAN: We should bring some home.

(The music upstairs is suddenly louder.)

(DAN starts to stand:)

DAN: I can tell them to be quiet.

CAT: It's fine. It's your last night. And you're the only guests. And—my parents aren't here. *(She smiles.)*

DAN: Right.

CAT: I'll go and make sure they're using the ashtrays.

DAN: That's a good idea.

EMILY: I love your accent. It's so sweet.

(CAT smiles and heads upstairs.)

EMILY: *(To DAN)* Don't you love her accent? She sounds so smart.

(Lights are out.)

(YOUNG MAN turns to the audience:)

YOUNG MAN: The music got louder. They danced. Henry brought out the bottle of vodka he had hidden in his bag. The oregano or birdseed wasn't oregano or birdseed after all. Cat supplied potato chips, sold them beer and danced. And so at least an hour passed before Emily's roommate suddenly appeared, her face red, her hands shaking, tears cascading down her cheeks. *Where I Come From.* Scene Two Emma Upset.

Scene Two

(EMMA *[17] Stands before* EMILY *and* DAN; *she is sobbing and trying to talk.*)

EMMA: I don't know what to do. I don't want... Oh God...

EMILY: *(Taking her hand)* Emma, please. I can't answer. Tell us.

DAN: Tell us, Emma. What happened?

(EMMA *breaks down sobbing.*)

EMILY: Let's wash your face. *(To* DAN*)* I'll take her to the bathroom.

(EMILY *helps* EMMA *off:*)

EMILY: Come on. You can tell us later. Let's get some cold water on that face...

(EMILY *and* EMMA *are gone.*)

(DAN *turns and sees* RICHARD *and* JANE, *holding hands, having watched this.*)

JANE: We heard... What's???

(DAN *shrugs.*)

(*Lights fade.*)

YOUNG MAN: *(To us)* Some time passed. News spread upstairs. Then finally the girls returned from the bathroom…

(Lights up)

(RICHARD *and* JANE *have been joined by* BECCA *and* JAMES. *Music loud off as the dancing continues.)*

(EMILY *tries to comfort* EMMA.)

JANE: I don't understand. Who's she talking about?

RICHARD: *(To* JANE) Mr Alexander.

JANE: Mr Alexander.

YOUNG MAN: *(To us)* Mr Alexander was one of the teachers along on this trip.

EMMA: *(Trying not to cry)* He… *(To* EMILY) I told you—

EMILY: *(Over this)* You don't have to—

DAN: Maybe we should leave her alone.

EMILY: *(Over this)* I'll tell them. *(To the others)* Mr. Alexander and Emma, they were walking to the theatre—they were lost. Just the two of them?

(EMMA *nods.)*

EMILY: And they're crossing a little bridge and he puts his arm around her. And hugs her. Then asks for a bigger hug. And he holds her against him. Puts his face against her neck. She tried to push him… Right?

EMMA: I did.

EMILY: And he put his hand? He tried to touch your breasts?

EMMA: *(Shrugs)* I think so. It happened so… *(To the others)* But I pushed him away! And then he said: don't tell anyone about this. Forget it.

EMILY: And he walked off. They were lost and he walked off.

JANE: I don't believe this. I like Mr. Alexander.

YOUNG MAN: *(To us)* He taught American history. He was nearly fifty. Two grown children. A wife.

(HENRY, KATHY, and LIBBY enter.)

KATHY: What's—?

RICHARD: Sh-sh. We'll tell you. *(To DAN)* She should talk to your father, Dan.

DAN: I'll take her. He'll know what to—

EMILY: She's been to him.

DAN: What??

KATHY: *(Whispers to JANE)* What's going—?

(JANE whispers to KATHY as:)

EMILY: That's where she's been. She went to Mr. Williams right away. Like she thought she was supposed to do. This was during the play?

EMMA: At the intermission.

EMILY: I think that's why he's been so—angry tonight.

RICHARD: Why be angry at us?

EMILY: I don't know. Anyway, you told him. He said not to tell anyone yet, right? To come to see him after, and you went.

(EMMA nods.)

KATHY: *(Hearing what JANE has been whispering)* Oh my God. Shit.

EMILY: *(Continuing)* And he tells her, 'are you sure about this? Maybe there's been a misunderstanding. Maybe Mr Alexander was worried that you were col, Emma. It's a cold night out.'

(EMILY looks at DAN who shakes his head; he cannot believe this.)

EMILY: Then she says, she's sure, right?

(EMMA *sniffles. Someone hands her a tissue from* EMILY'*s box.* RICHARD *hands her a beer.*)

(*Then* RICHARD *just stares at* EMMA *and she finally says:*)

EMMA: (*Quietly*) "Do you know how hard this is for me? Jack Alexander is a friend. Do you know what this could do to this man? You want to destroy his career?"

KATHY: (*Disgusted*) Oh my God.

EMMA: (*After a sip of beer*) "Destroy—his family? His life?? And that's when I started crying and I couldn't stop. And he started yelling at me: Jack says you said you were cold, Emma! "You told him?" I said. "I had to. What did you think?"

EMILY: And then he called Mr Alexander into the room with them. He was waiting right outside.

(DAN *suddenly walks away from everyone.*)

LIBBY: It's not your fault, Dan. It isn't.

(BILL *followed by* CAT *is entering.* KATHY *grabs them and whispers as:*)

EMILY: So Mr Williams says to Emma—

EMMA: "Accuse him, Emma. There he is, accuse him to his face." I look up and you can tell he's really angry at me. Then he says in a very dead voice, "Emma you missed the first act of the play tonight. You knew you were going to be punished. To say things like this, that's not going to help you. It's wrong." (*Pause*) Then Mr Williams said, "If you can't accuse him to his face, then I think you should get out of here." So I started to leave, and he grabs my wrist and holds it and says, "We all make mistakes. Let's forget this whole thing, okay? Let's even forget you were late for the play, okay?" And then I saw Mr Alexander wink at him and he let go and I went out into the hall. They closed the door and I could hear Mr Alexander say things about me. About what he says he's heard about me… The kind of person… *(She starts to sob.)* I don't know what to do…I don't know what…

(EMILY tries to hug EMMA, EMMA moves away. Looks at DAN, slowly goes to him. and hits him on the shoulder and shouts:)

EMMA: I hate your father! I hate him!

(Others grab EMMA and hold her.)

(Lights fade.)

YOUNG MAN: *(To us)* No one turned the music off upstairs. They let it play. At first no one knew what to say, then more beers where found, more potato chips. And they grouped themselves in front of the comforting warmth of the small gas fire and listened to each other talk. *Where I Come From.* Scene Three. Group Portrait.

Scene Three

(Music from upstairs. Everyone sits on the couch, chairs, or on the floor in fron of the gas fire [unseen]. and they talk. Every now and then someone gets up to get another beer or go to the bathroom. One or two smoke, etc.)

LIBBY: Cat, I can't believe your parents just…

CAT: Nothing's going to happen. No one's going to— hurt anything.

LIBBY: I wasn't saying… *(She shrugs.)* They trust you.

(CAT nods. Others nod at this thought. LIBBY sips her beer.)

LIBBY: I don't think I'm ready to go home yet. *(Smiles to herself.)* Everyone's going to sleep on the plane. Coming over here, no one slept. That first day—like everything in slow motion. The whole day. *(Another sip)* I miss my dog. I think that's all I miss. Becca here missed everything.

BECCA: That's not true. Stop that. Shut up.

LIBBY: You cried—

BECCA: I said shut up.

KATHY: She hugged her little stuffed rabbit—

BECCA: Go to hell.

JANE: It's all right. What's the weather like at home. Snowing?

LIBBY: No.

BECCA: She talks to her mother every day.

JANE: So what? Leave her alone.

EMILY: I talk to my stepmother too. I've never been away from home before too.

LIBBY: How did she know that I have never been—?

EMILY: It's okay.

(Short pause)

(Music is heard.)

DAN: Anyone going to turn that [the music] off?

EMILY: *(Continuing)* It's a funny feeling though being so far away—thousands of miles away. You can't like just run home.

(EMILY looks at EMMA who is next to her, and strokes her arm.)

EMILY: I think my Dad was more worried than I was.

KATHY: My Dad was worried too. He kept giving me more money on the way to the airport. Sometimes I think he's the handsomest man in the world. And sometimes I think he's a pathetic jerk.

(Others girls nod at this: their feelings about their fathers too.)

KATHY: Weird. He took me to look at his old college? Maybe for me to go there? *(Shakes her head, amazed: she'd never go there.)* He was like all nervous. We're walking outside—*outside* and he's whispering. And I say, Dad, why are you whispering for God's sake? I'll never go to his college. I'd never hear the end of it. Like I'm supposed to be him? He wanted to show me all the places—where he—whatever... *(She plays with the potoato chips.)* I tried to explain to my mother but she can't hear it. She just defends him, so... *(Shrugs)* Not defends, she wouldn't think that way— 'explains' as if you're two years old.

LIBBY: I know what you—

KATHY: He'll be five hours early at the airport. Sometimes he sits in the car, waiting for me to go somewhere, anywhere, and I purposely take longer, just to let him sit. He's not going to tell me what to do.

BECCA: No.

JANE: My Dad's always late. I don't think he listens. Mom always has to tell him three times—anything. I don't know where his mind is. You can snap your fingers in his face and still...

JAMES: Thank God we have cars.

JANE: What?

KATHY: Why?

JAMES: *(On the spot)* So—we don't have to wait for our—parents?

KATHY: Jane doesn't have a car. Neither does—

JAMES: I know. I know. I meant—me.

EMMA: My Mother says Kathy's Dad's pretty cool. She does.

KATHY: Sometimes he is.

EMILY: *(Over this)* What, she's hitting on your Dad?

(Laughter)

EMMA: I don't think my Mom is hitting on any guy.

EMILY: Right. Sorry, I—

EMMA: Don't be sorry. She just thinks he's cool. Thinks he's funny.

(Pause)

(They sip their beers, etc.)

LIBBY: My Mother said—you may never get to Europe again. So make the most of it, dear. Why did she have to say that? Why does she say things like that? She's never been to Europe. She loves to put pressure on—

JAMES: And they turn it around so it's about them...

(Agreement)

JAMES: Their thing or success or problem. Or how they will be 'seen'. They always do that.

HENRY: Ever catch your parents having sex? What about you, Dan?

EMILY: Leave him alone—

JANE: I have.

BILL: I don't think Dan's Father has sex—

HENRY: He must have had to once—

BILL: Maybe.

(They laugh and are ignored by the others.)

JANE: *(Continuing)* I caught mine once. I don't know what my Dad was doing home. It was in the afternoon. We only had a half day of school, so I...I was already home, in my room, when I heard them come in...I was

about to say something when… you know, they went
at it. Big time.

RICHARD: In the bedroom?

JANE: In the rec room. On the couch. From my room
I could see them downstairs. It's not something a kid
should see.

OTHERS: *(Agree:)* No.

BECCA: When I was maybe eight or nine. We were in a
motel room. On some stupid trip. God knows where.
I remember my Father always wanting to show me
a map and tell me this is where—. We are or been or
something.

EMILY: I know I hate that.

BECCA: Anyway some stupid 'family trip.'

BILL: Those are the worst. I run like hell when I hear
'family trip'—

BECCA: *(Continuing)* I have a bed and they have a bed.
Actually my Mom slept with me, cause I couldn't
sleep—but then I realized later—

JANE: To *get* you asleep.

BECCA: Right. So she must think I'm out and she slowly
gets out of my bed, but I'm lying on my side, so I can
see, Dad's looking at her, and from under the cover he
is pulling off his pajama bottoms, Mom's taking off her
nightgown over her head, and I'm watching through a
slit in my eyes, then I can't move or anything or they'd
notice, so… *(Sips her beer.)* Yuch.

RICHARD: Thy should have got another room.

LIBBY: Yeh.

JAMES: That doesn't work either. I was with my
brothers and we were visiting my Uncle in New York
City. So we got two hotel rooms, one for my parents

and the other for—us. To do what *we* want in. Jump on the beds, watch T V all night. I don't know what they thought but you could hear everything through the wall. *(He makes sounds of a bed banging against the wall. Then makes orgasim sounds that are gross.)*

KATHY: Stop it!

JAMES: *(Continues)* I thought my brothers would pee in their pants. They didn't know what was going on. I told them Mom must have got a splinter and Dad was helping get it out. Parents are clueless. I thought they were supposed to protect us from…? I don't know. But Jesus Christ— *(Starts the sound again)*

BECCA: We said stop that!

LIBBY: I caught my Father once come home so completely drunk. He couldn't talk. Just looked away from… Looked like he was angry at me.

CAT: I've seen my Father drunk many many times.

(They glance at CAT *who has joined in for the first time, then back at each other.)*

BILL: And when you catch *them* in a lie, they hate that, don't they? It's like it's your fault, that you Should—

EMILY: My step-mom's pretty neat, I think. She should have been my Mom. I don't' know what she sees in my Dad.

BILL: She is neat.

JANE: He thinks so because she wears jeans so tight you can see the crack in her pussy.

BILL: That is one reason.

(Laughter)

EMILY: I'm trying to get her to spend more time with me. I think she feels she doesn't want to—get in between or something. I don't understand.

KATHY: I've never even seen my parents kiss.

(This stops everyone.)

JANE: What?

KATHY: On the lips. I haven't. Maybe they do. Maybe they don't.

BILL: Maybe she just likes to suck him off.

JANE: Shut up.

LIBBY: My Mother said to me—dear, you may never get this chance to go to Europe again so—

EMMA: You already told us that.

EMILY: Talking about tongue kissing—

RICHARD: Who was talking about—?

EMILY: Anyone else have an Uncle who—?

JANE: Tongue kisses??

EMILY: Almost. It's what he wants to do. You feel that.

LIBBY: How do you feel that?

EMILY: He'd wet his lips just before—. And I think he wants me to see him wetting his lips… Then the look in his eyes as he kisses…

JANE: I had an 'uncle' in quotes—a friend of my Mom's. I think she'd dated him in college. I was maybe like twelve just starting to get breasts—

BECCA: I'm still waiting for mine!

(Laughter)

JANE: And we're in the swimming pool, he likes suddenly swims under me, then he pops up out of the water, and he like pressed against me and the side of the pool. He looked down and so I looked and you could tell he had this big hard on in his trunks.

KATHY: You were twelve and you knew what a 'hard on' was—?

JANE: I have an older sister.

KATHY: Did you tell your mother?

JANE: Tell her what? He didn't *do* anything. It was only a couple of years later that I realized… That he was seeing what I 'knew', where I—'was.'

BECCA: Sometimes you think it's just you.

EMMA: I know. I know.

(Others realize the more immediate meaning of EMMA's *agreement, but continue:)*

HENRY: I wanted to learn to swim. And there was a Y. But my Father wouldn't take me, my Mother told me it was because he didn't like taking his clothes off in front of men. For some reason I remember she found that really funny. Why?

(Others shrug.)

BILL: I don't know.

HENRY: So she took me. Sent me into the dressing room by myself. I don't know. I don't' remember any one thing that happened. But I never wanted to go bak there.

LIBBY: I think by law mothers should be made to wear only *one*-piece bathing suits.

GIRLS: I agree!

BILL: Not step-mothers!

LIBBY: Not step-mothers. I went shopping once with my Mother to buy me a new bathing suit—

BECCA: That—I would never do. I'd rather pull out my eyes—

LIBBY: *(Over this)* And she started trying on all these—.
I said to her, you're not a kid, Mom. And that made it
worse.

BECCA: It would. Why didn't you know that?

LIBBY: So she bought this bikini. *(She shakes her head.
Takes a big sip from her beer.)* She didn't even know
about shaving her hair…

EMILY: She must have known—

LIBBY: If she did, she hadn't done it. Christ. I thought
I was going to throw up. I couldn't look at her. And
she was so happy with herself. Kept smiling at me.
Grinning.

EMILY: My Mother once took me swimming in the
reservoir. She said she wanted a kind of 'mother-
daughter' memory.

JANE: Uh-oh. That usually means trouble.

BECCA: True.

EMILY: So we're swimming in this sort-of lake, we
get out to the middle and a little floating—dock, you
know, with a diving board on it, we're hanging onto
it, and she says—the sun's in my eyes now, so I can
hardly see her face—she has planned this. So she
says—she hates—my father. The things he's done to
her, she won't go into—, because she knows I'll still
have to see him, if I wish. If I'm stupid enough is
the implication. If I can stomach it, which—she can't
anymore. But she understands he's my—but he's
fucking anything that walks. Her words. So how much
time will he really have for me? So—. She's leaving
him. Actually he was leaving her, but I only learn this
later. Leaving him. Now I'm in the middle of a lake.
This is all a plan, so I can't just walk away and slam my
door. I hated her for that. For doing that to me. From
taking that away—of just slamming my goddamn

door. I just started swimming back. So we drove home and I said shit to her. That's why I think I stayed with my Father for the first six months or so. Even though I hated that, I knew he didn't want me, he made that clear, but I wanted to punish my Mother for telling me like that.

(Pause)

EMMA: I got one of those.

BILL: So do I—

BECCA: Let Emma...

(Short pause)

*(*EMMA *takes her time to get settled, then:)*

EMMA: When Mom told me she and Dad—. My Dad wouldn't tell me anything. He just looked at me and shook his head. What does that mean? What did I do?

BILL: I know I—

EMMA: So then she says—remember Barbara? And there's—Barbara, this woman who was part of our book club that Mom made us go to—so we could be—I don't know. She had something in mind. God did I hate it. Barbara. She's a lawyer in town. She's going to be staying with us, Mom says. What does that mean? I don't say this, but...

EMILY: Sure.

EMMA: Yeh. Where's she going to sleep, Mom? There's only my room. This makes her laugh and she, and Barbara now too I see in my bedroom doorway, and she is laughing and nodding and giving me a real 'sweet' look. Fuck her. Barbara, Mom says, will sleep on the pullout couch. But then—she didn't. They made up the couch for her that one night and no one slept on it. She and Mom... *(Sips her beer.)* Why do we have to guess at everything?

(Pause)

(Music plays upstairs.)

(Someone goes to get a few more beers.)

(Then:)

EMMA: Barbara's okay. She's done nothing to me.

BECCA: Why can't they just talk to us?

BILL: Right.

KATHY: I don't want to talk to my parents.

CAT: Me neither.

RICHARD: Shit, no.

BILL: When Dad got married the third time—they say the third wife and the first wife usually hit it off? I read that in a book. That didn't happen. I was trying to figure out what was going to happen. Anyway—every time they argue I now think—that's it. That's over. So I try to get it into my head, into my skin. So they'll be no—shock?? Then in the morning—after the fight?—it's like nothing has happened? Well something has happened to me. I just want to know—what I can feel.

(Pause)

(New beers are brought.)

(Music plays upstairs.)

HENRY: We left the music—

JANE: We'll go back.

RICHARD: No one's going to sleep tonight.

HENRY: I don't think so.

(Pause)

KATHY: What time is it in Ardmore?

HENRY: Ten.

(Pause)

KATHY: I wonder if they're talking about us. Our parents.

HENRY: Some are and some aren't.

BECCA: I like my parents.

BILL: Good for you. You're lucky.

KATHY: I like her parents too. They're neat.

BILL: Is everyone packed?

JANE: Maybe we should dance?

BECCA: I'd like to be like my Mom.

LIBBY: I miss my parents too. I'm looking forward to going home. I hate being so far away.

(There is a shift in tone, the conversation gets suddenly more lively:)

KATHY: I bought my Dad a tie. It's the only thing I ever buy him. I think I looked for about two hours in that little tie store. I got one with the Queen. He lies ties.

JANE: I got my parents these cute coasters from the Tate? Did you see them?

(Others have.)

HENRY: Who was the artist, I keep—?

EMILY: Blake.

JANE: I think they'll really like them. They always like what I give them.

JAMES: My parents too. They like whatever—

JANE: I always used to make things—

BECCA: Me too.

KATHY: Art stuff from school.

RICHARD: Yeh.

JANE: They keep everything I think. Somewhere.

(Short pause)

RICHARD: I remember the first time I was away from
my parents. I had like a babysitter or a friend of theirs
or something. And they were going out—for dinner?
Maybe they just told me this, but supposedly they say I
could throw up whenever I…I could cry, make my face
turn red and then throw up. So the last thing they'd
see as they were closing the front door was me puking.
That got them. That really got them.

JANE: When was this last summer?

RICHARD: When I was like three or something. Shut up.

KATHY: My Dad cried at the airport.

LIBBY: I cried at the airport.

JANE: So did I.

KATHY: It seems so far away.

EMILY: And everything here, it's so different. It is Cat.
It really is.

JANE: She'll have to come and visit—

CAT: No, I don't think—

BECCA: You will. You have to.

EMILY: It's different, but then it's sort of similar, and
that's really confusing.

EMMA: I know what you mean.

BILL: *(Over this)* I remember playing cards with my Dad
every night. Or some game. Then I bet him at chess
and he got really pissed at me. *(Laughs at the memory)*

JANE: I want my Mother's chin. I love her chin. She's
got a little dimple…

KATHY: What did you get your parents?

(The lights start to fade, as they all begin to talk at once:)

HENRY: I got postcards from that Portrait Museum. My Dad likes real pictures—Pictures of real things.

BECCA: *(Over this)* A scarf for my Mom, and for my Dad one of those magnets of the Tower Bridge—

LIBBY: I got a little notebook with Princess Di on the—

RICHARD: My Mother wanted some biscuits, she said I can get them at the airport—.

(And the lights are out.)

YOUNG MAN: *(To us)* After awhile, they grew tired of talking, and leaving Emma, Emily and Dad once again alone, they went upstairs—to dance.

Scene Four

(From upstairs: music and dancing is heard, kids shouting with the music as they dance, etc.)

(DAN, EMILY, and EMMA sit. They eat chips, drink both beer and vodka. All three are a bit drunk.)

EMMA: I've waited too long to call my Mother. I'll have to wait until I get home to tell her...

EMILY: About Mr—?

(EMMA nods.)

(Short pause)

DAN: *(Finally)* Maybe that's best.

EMILY: Why?

DAN: What can her mother do now? It's—

(DAN looks at his watch and shows EMILY.)

Wake up my Father and scream at him? What's that going to achieve?

(Short pause)

EMILY: I don't think that's the point—to achieve something. I think it'd be nice to know someone is fighting for you. So you're not alone.

(DAN *shrugs.*)

DAN: I don't know. It's…

(DAN *shows* EMILY *his watch again.*)

DAN: *(Turns to* EMMA*)* Do you feel alone?

(EMMA *nods.*)

EMILY: See?

(DAN *takes a sip of his vodka. Music is suddenly loud upstairs.*)

YOUNG MAN: *(To us) Where I Come From.* Scene Four. Sex.

(EMILY *suddenly stands:*)

EMILY: I've a couple of pictures I still have to take. What about one of Emma and me?

EMMA: No! Not like this, I must look—

EMILY: You look fine. Doesn't she?

DAN: Sure—

EMILY: I'm the one who's sick.

DAN: You seem a lot better, do you—?

EMILY: I'm fine. Take the two of us. Come on.

(DAN *takes the camera.* EMILY *and* EMMA *sit together on the couch.*)

DAN: Sit still. A little closer. One. Two. Three.

(Flash)

(EMMA *jumps up.*)

EMMA: One of the two of you. You're best friends.

DAN: I don't need…

EMILY: You don't need what?

DAN: Do *you* want—??

EMMA: Come on. Get closer. Put your arm around her Dan. That's better. Emily sit like that girl in the play.

DAN: The one that Henry liked?

EMILY: I didn't see the play, remember. I'm—

EMMA: Put your legs… Dan, put her legs…

(DAN *takes* EMILY's *legs and puts them across his legs.*)

EMMA: *(Going up to* EMILY*)* And pull up your skirt.

EMILY: Emma!

(DAN *playfully tickles* EMILY's *knee.*)

EMILY: Stop that! I'm sick.

EMMA: Shut up. One. Two. A little closer. Dan.

(*Suddenly* DAN *puts his face close to* EMILY's *and* EMMA *takes the photo:*)

EMMA: Three!

(*Flash*)

EMILY: *(To Dan, moving her legs)* What are you doing?

DAN: *(To* EMMA*)* How many are left?

EMMA: One more. *(To* EMILY*)* One more?

DAN: Of me and Emma. Come on.

(DAN *takes* EMMA *by the hand. She almost falls over.*)

EMMA: I tripped. Where should—?

EMILY: On the couch. Come on. And get real close.

EMMA: Like this?

(EMMA *puts her arms around* DAN *and gives him a big kiss on the cheek.*)

DAN: Emma—

EMILY: Do it again. Let me get that.

(EMMA *agressively takes* DAN'*s head and kisses him on the mouth.*)

EMILY: One. Two.

(DAN *pushes* EMMA *off, she immediately goes for his ear with her mouth to kiss that. On the count of:*)

EMILY: Three!

(*Flash and* EMMA *starts to wretch; she is going to be sick to her stomach.*)

DAN: Shit.

EMMA: (*Holding her mouth*) I'm going to be sick.

EMILY: Get to the bathroom. Come on, get up—

(EMMA *starts to get up, she holds her stomach and begins to dry heave.*)

EMILY: You'll be fine. Come on. I'll take you to the bathroom.

(EMILY *and* EMMA *are gone.*)

(*Music is heard.* DAN *stands not knowing what to do. After a few moments,* EMILY *returns.*)

EMILY: She made it.

DAN: Shouldn't you—

EMILY: No one wants company when…

DAN: She drank too much.

EMILY: Yeh. (*Short pause*) She won't be the only one. On the flight home, a lot of people are… Listen.

(*The dancing upstairs*)

EMILY: (*She rubs her face.*) I should go to bed.

DAN: Me too.

EMILY: We shouldn't leaver her…

DAN: No. You go and I'll…

EMILY: No. No. She's… She got it on her blouse. She took off her blouse. I should stay. *(Short pause)* I don't blame her one bit. Getting drunk.

DAN: Me neither. *(He smiles.)*

EMILY: What are you smiling about?

DAN: She had her tongue in my ear?

EMILY: What??

DAN: She stuck her tongue in my ear. Just now. Then she started…heaving. *(Laughs a little)* Ever had a tongue in your ear, it's weird.

EMILY: No. I haven't. *(Looks at DAN and smiles)* She must like you.

DAN: I don't think—

EMILY: *(Teasing)* I think she does.

DAN: Come on. Leave her alone, she's gone through enough today.

EMILY: You brought up the tongue. *(She straightens her skirt.)* I have hips like a boy's.

DAN: What are you talking about?

EMILY: I was just looking at my hips.

DAN: You're thin. That's good, isn't it? Isn't that what you want to be?

EMILY: I don't know.

DAN: I like your hips.

EMILY: Forget it! I was talking to myself. I'm sorry I—. *(New thought)* I should call my Step-mom and tell her what time the flight gets in.

DAN: Doesn't she know that? It was on the sheet the parents—

EMILY: I can tell her I forgot.

DAN: It's really late. You could scare her. I know if I called my Mom—

EMILY: I'll say I got the time wrong...

(DAN *looks at* EMILY *and shrugs.*)

EMILY: Do you parents know when you're lying? I can't tell about mien. Sometimes they seem to know everything. Then...I can tell them the biggest lie—. They just accept. I don't get it.

DAN: Maybe they just don't want to catch you. Sometimes I think they're more worried about catching you than what you're lying about.

EMILY: I don't understand.

DAN: They don't want to know. Sometimes. They really don't. Least that's what I think. In my house we're never saying what we really are—thinking.

EMILY: I guess that's true with me too. (*Smiles at him*) You know it can't be easy for you—being the teacher's kid. Everyone watching... You handle it okay. You do.

DAN: Thanks.

EMILY: I should check on... I'll be right back. (*She goes and returns in a moment.*) She's asleep. On the floor in there. Poor girl. I can't leave her, but I don't want to move her upstairs...

DAN: You're right. You'll sleep on the plane.

EMILY: Yeh.

(*Pause*)

DAN: What are you thinking?

EMILY: I hate that question. My dad always asks me that. What are you supposed to say?

DAN: I'm sorry.

EMILY: Why are you apologizing?! Christ. *(She looks at him, then:)* Never mind. It was just that you suddenly reminded me of my Father. Forget it. It's in my head. It's my problem. Put your arm around me.

(DAN does.)

EMILY: And don't say anything.

(Pause)

(DAN obviously wants to talk but feels like he shouldn't, until:)

EMILY: Hand me some potato chips.

(DAN does. One drops on EMILY's lap. He wipes it off; he allows his hand to linger; then removes it; she takes it and holds it.)

DAN: *(To say something)* Becca lost her passport today.

EMILY: Did she?

YOUNG MAN: *(To us)* It would take another hour, but Dan would kiss Emily—on the lips. And she would immediately kiss him back.

DAN: Yeh. It became this real big deal. My Father went berserk. He went to the Embassy with her. He missed half the show. That's how Mr. Alexander ended up—. He wasn't with my Father.

EMILY: So what happened with the passport? Did she get another one?

YOUNG MAN: *(To us)* They danced here in the sitting room. They turned off the lamps. He slid his hand under her blouse and touched her. She pressed herself against him, and felt him.

DAN: She found it in her raincoat. There's an inner pocket in her raincoat. She was wearing it. At the Embassy. She just pulls it out, I'm told. I don't think she's going to get a very good grade for this course.

(DAN *and* EMILY *laugh.*)

YOUNG MAN: *(To us)* He unbuttoned two buttons of her blouse. She did the rest. She undid his belt and with her thumb and forefinger she pulled down the zipper of his pants.

DAN: Becca tried to cry when she saw how angry Dad was. But Dad just walked away from her. And she stopped—liked that. Amazing.

EMILY: That's Becca. I've seen her pull that with her parents.

(DAN *looks at* EMILY.)

EMILY: What?

DAN: I've been wondering—if you brought a stuffed animal too, with you like Becca and her—

EMILY: Rabbit? *(Pretending to be "tough")* And what if I did, buster? *(She touches his chest with her fingers.)* His name is Anthony. *(Almost in baby-talk:)* And he protects me. He's as koala bear. And I love him.

YOUNG MAN: *(To us)* Once that night, as she sat on him with him inside, they heard a noise. Someone coming through. It was Emma, sniffling as she shuffled up to bed. To keep him from speaking, Emily covered Dan's lips with her own.

EMILY: And the man I marry, he's going to have to just face it that Anthony's coming with me and he's sleeping in our bed.

(DAN *nods "seriously", then:)*

DAN: Exactly how big is he?

(DAN *smiles,* EMILY *laughs and "hits" him playfully.*)

(*Lights fade.*)

Scene Five

YOUNG MAN: *(To us)* Morning. *Where I Come From.*
Scene Five. Heading Home.

*(Morning light. The room is empty. No music plays off.
Then the students begin entering with their suitcases. They
are all tired, sleepy, even hungover.)*

*(*BECCA, KATHY, *and* LIBBY *enter with* CAT.*)*

BECCA: *(Entering)* You'll love it there. And we have the
room. My parents love guests. Especially when they're
from some place—exotic.

CAT: I wouldn't call England—

BECCA: My parents would. I'll show you all the neat
places to hang out. Philadelphia isn't as bad as it first
seems.

*(*KATHY *makes a face.)*

(Pushing KATHY*)* Come on. If you know where to go.

BECCA: If you go to—

ALL THREE: South Street.

CAT: I'll ask my parents, but I'm sure they'll—

(As they start to exit off, RICHARD *enters from that
direction:)*

RICHARD: Mr Williams says to wait in here. Until the
cabs come. It's raining.

LIBBY: What a surprise.

BECCA: *(Continuing the conversation with* CAT*)* Tell them
it'll be educational. That always gets them.

*(*JANE *enters without a suitcase.)*

JANE: *(To* RICHARD*)* What did you do with my bags?

RICHARD: They're on the stoop.

*(*JANE *starts to go.)*

RICHARD: We're supposed to wait in here.

(JANE, *obviously exhausted, nods, and leans against a chair or couch.*)

BECCA: *(To* JANE*)* Cat's coming to visit. She's going to stay with me.

CAT: I have to ask—

JANE: Great. We can show her what a 'shower' is. *(Laughs to herself at her joke)*

CAT: What do you mean?

KATHY: Ignore her. She's stupid.

(BILL, DAN, HENRY, *and* JAMES *enter with their bags.*)

JANE: *(Making "fun" of the "news")* Cat's coming to America!

BILL: Why?

JAMES: Now?

CAT: No, maybe in the summer when school's out—

LIBBY: You know how much vacation they get here? Like a week and a half.

CAT: It's as little more than.

JANE: We'll teach her about water pressure and vacations and—

HENRY: And hamburgers.

CAT: We have—

HENRY: No, you don't. You don't know. Trust me.

(RICHARD *takes as few of the girls' bags off.*)

EMILY: *(Hurries in)* Has anyone seen my green scarf? I can't find it anywhere upstairs.

BILL: *(Obviously not listening)* What color is it?

EMILY: Green.

BILL: No.

EMILY: What color scarf have you seen?

BILL: I haven't seen any scarf. What are you talking about?

(EMILY *starts back upstairs.*)

DAN: You want some help?

(DAN *and* EMILY *share a look, then she shakes her head and as she goes, she bumps into* EMMA.)

EMMA: Is everyone as—tired as I am?

(*Most everyone groans in agreement.*)

HENRY: We're supposed to wait in—

EMMA: I don't care. Sh-sh. (She drops her bags down and breathes deeply. Pause What are we doing?

LIBBY: *(Shrugs)* Waiting.

KATHY: *(quietly)* Goodbye little B and B! You are so—authentic!

DAN: Shouldn't we pay Cat for some of the beer and food last night—?

HENRY: I thought we did.

DAN: Not for everything.

CAT: *(Over this)* It's all right. It's fine. It's okay, I—

HENRY: Give me your change, Bill. What do you have left?

(*They start giving* CAT *their change.*)

LIBBY: We don't pay for the taxi or do we?

DAN: It's part of the whole deal.

JAMES: Here's—fifty pence. That's fifty right?

BILL: I've got a—two. This big one.

DAN: *(Reading it)* It's two pence.

BILL: Is that okay?

(As CAT *reluctantly colllects their change:)*

BECCA: Goodbye England. Goodbye Cartwright Gardens. Goodbye—

LIBBY: All those plays. Whatever they were called.

BECCA: *(To* EMMA*)* Cat's going to visit.

EMMA: Good. Don't stay with her *(*BECCA*)*. You'll never see anything. Stay with us. We've got a pullout couch that no one uses.

(Pause. Everyone waits.)

YOUNG MAN: *(To us)* And so—they went home. Where Jane and—

*(*RICHARD *comes in and grabs a few more bags and goes.)*

YOUNG MAN: Richard will soon split up. That will be big news. *(Then:)* And Emma—she will never tell her mother what had happened with her and the teacher. There will never seem to be the right moment, until too much time will pass and she'll know that she'd have to explain that as well. Mr. Alexander in school will treat her as he always had treated her—as if nothing had happened. She will cry herself to sleep many a night. *(Then:)* Kathy's father will be waiting at the airport when they arrive. He'll have been there about three hours early. *(Then:)* Jane's dad will be late. Mr Williams will be forced to wait with her until he shows up.

*(*RICHARD *hurries back in.)*

RICHARD: The taxis are here. Let's go.

EVERYONE: *(To* CAT*:)* Goodbye, Goodbye.

CAT: *(Helping with the luggage)* We'll say our goodbyes outside.

(As they all go:)

DAN: I'll wait for Emily. She'll be right down.

(All go except for DAN.*)*

YOUNG MAN: *(To us)* And Dan and Emily? They will soon learn that they had conceived a baby that night. In this room. On that couch—or one very much like it.

*(*EMILY *enters holding her scarf.)*

EMILY: It *was* under the bed. I'd looked three times. I would have been so upset…

*(*DAN *and* EMILY *smile at each other. An awkward moment as he hesitantly kisses her on the cheek. She starts to put on her scarf as:)*

YOUNG MAN: *(To us)* They will return to a storm of outrage by their parents. There will be a desperate attempt at self-abortion. There will be tears and screams and accusations made. And there will be cries and the almost continuous whispers of adults throughout the long and lonely nights. *(Then:)* Then nine months later a boy will be born. And they will name me Michael.

EMILY: *(As they go off)* We're coming. *(With as glance back:)* Goodbye…

(They are gone.)

(The YOUNG MAN *goes and sits on the couch.)*

END OF PLAY

www.ingramcontent.com/pod-product-compliance
Lightning Source LLC
Chambersburg PA
CBHW070035110426
42741CB00035B/2781